The Lovely Bones

Copyright © 2024 by Talha Iqbal All rights reserved. No part of this publication may be reproduced, distributed, or transmitted in any form or by any means, including photocopying, recording, or other electronic or mechanical methods, without the prior written permission of the author, except in the case of brief quotations embodied in critical reviews and certain other noncommercial uses permitted by copyright law.

Contents

Innocence Shattered 4
A Family in Turmoil 7
The Afterlife Revealed 10
Searching for Justice 13
Glimpses of Hope 15
The Bonds of Love 18
A Father's Quest 21
The Perils of Obsession 23
Healing Through Connection 26
Closure and Acceptance 28

Innocence Shattered

The Tragic Disappearance

"The Lovely Bones," directed by Peter Jackson and based on Alice Sebold's novel, opens with the idyllic suburban life of the Salmon family in Pennsylvania during the 1970s. The picturesque setting, with its lush green lawns and cheerful households, sets the stage for a tale of innocence and its abrupt loss. The Salmon family consists of loving parents, Jack and Abigail, and their children, including Susie, a bright and imaginative young girl on the cusp of adolescence.

The film takes its first steps into darkness when Susie Salmon, portrayed by Saoirse Ronan, goes missing on her way home from school. Her disappearance sends shockwaves through the community and shatters the innocence of her family and friends. The initial moments of panic and confusion among the Salmons and their neighbors reflect the abrupt intrusion of tragedy into their lives. The once serene neighborhood becomes a place haunted by fear and uncertainty.

As the search for Susie intensifies, the film delves into the emotional turmoil experienced by her family. Jack, played by Mark Wahlberg, struggles to maintain composure while desperately searching for his daughter. Abigail, portrayed by Rachel Weisz, grapples with overwhelming grief, torn between hope and despair. Their other children, Lindsey and Buckley, also navigate the bewildering reality of their sister's disappearance, each coping in their own way.

In the midst of this chaos, Susie's narrative voice emerges, providing a unique perspective from beyond the grave. From her heavenly vantage point, Susie recounts the events leading up to her disappearance and observes the impact of her absence on those she left behind. Through her eyes, the audience gains insight into the inner thoughts and emotions of the characters, adding depth to their experiences.

The theme of shattered innocence permeates the film as Susie's once-secure world is shattered by violence and cruelty. Her dreams and aspirations are cruelly cut short, leaving behind a void that can never be filled. The loss of innocence extends beyond Susie herself to encompass her family, whose lives are irrevocably changed by the tragedy.

As the days turn into weeks and months, the search for Susie yields few answers, leaving her family to grapple with the agonizing uncertainty of her fate. The passage of time only deepens their wounds, as they struggle to come to terms with the reality of her absence. The film captures the raw anguish of parental grief, as Jack and Abigail confront the possibility of never seeing their daughter again.

Amidst the darkness, glimmers of light emerge as the community rallies around the Salmon family in their time of need. Neighbors offer support and assistance, reflecting the resilience of the human spirit in the face of tragedy. Acts of kindness and compassion provide moments of solace amidst the overwhelming grief, demonstrating the power of community in times of crisis.

As the investigation into Susie's disappearance unfolds, suspicion falls on George Harvey, a reclusive neighbor played by Stanley Tucci. Harvey's sinister demeanor and suspicious behavior cast a shadow of doubt over the tight-knit community, fueling speculation about his possible involvement in Susie's disappearance. The revelation of Harvey's true nature exposes the dark underbelly of suburbia, challenging the notion of safety and security in the familiar surroundings of home.

Throughout the film, Susie's spirit remains a guiding presence, offering comfort and reassurance to her family as they navigate the turbulent waters of grief and loss. Her ethereal presence serves as a reminder of the enduring bond between loved ones, transcending the boundaries of life and death. In moments of despair, Susie's voice echoes through the darkness, providing a beacon of hope amidst the overwhelming darkness.

As the search for Susie reaches its conclusion, the Salmon family is forced to confront the harsh reality of her fate. The discovery of Susie's remains brings a sense of closure to her loved ones, allowing them to begin the long and painful process of healing. In the aftermath of tragedy, the Salmons find strength in their shared memories of Susie, cherishing the moments they shared together.

"Innocence Shattered: The Tragic Disappearance" serves as a poignant reminder of the fragility of life and the devastating impact of loss. Through the lens of the Salmon family's experience, the film explores themes of grief, resilience, and the enduring power of love. Despite the darkness that surrounds them, the Salmons emerge from their ordeal with a newfound sense of strength and resilience, honoring Susie's memory with each step they take forward.

A Family in Turmoil

Coping with Loss

"A Family in Turmoil: Coping with Loss," encapsulates the central theme that unfolds following Susie Salmon's disappearance. As the film progresses, it delves deeply into the emotional turmoil experienced by the Salmon family and their journey towards acceptance and healing in the wake of tragedy.

The Salmons, a seemingly ordinary suburban family, are thrust into a nightmare when Susie, their beloved daughter and sister, goes missing. The initial shock and disbelief give way to a profound sense of grief and despair as they come to terms with the reality of her disappearance. Each member of the family copes with their loss in their own way, navigating the complex and often tumultuous emotions that accompany such a profound tragedy.

At the heart of the family's turmoil is Jack Salmon, Susie's father, portrayed by Mark Wahlberg. Jack's world is shattered by the disappearance of his daughter, and he embarks on a relentless quest to find her, clinging to hope even as the days turn into weeks and months. His anguish is palpable as he grapples with the agonizing uncertainty of Susie's fate, torn between the need to find her and the crushing weight of despair.

Abigail Salmon, Susie's mother, played by Rachel Weisz, also struggles to cope with the loss of her daughter. Consumed by grief, Abigail retreats into herself, unable to find solace in the familiar routines of everyday life. Her anguish is compounded by feelings of guilt and helplessness, as she grapples with the belief that she failed to protect her daughter. Abigail's journey is one of profound transformation as she confronts her grief and seeks a path towards healing.

Lindsey Salmon, Susie's younger sister, portrayed by Rose McIver, also experiences the tumultuous aftermath of Susie's disappearance. While she initially grapples with feelings of anger and resentment towards her sister, Lindsey ultimately finds strength in their bond, determined to uncover the truth about what happened to Susie. Her resilience and determination serve as a source of inspiration for the family as they navigate the darkest moments of their grief.

Buckley Salmon, the youngest member of the family, is also deeply affected by Susie's disappearance. Unable to fully comprehend the magnitude of the tragedy, Buckley struggles to understand why his sister is gone. His innocence serves as a stark reminder of the profound impact that Susie's loss has on the entire family, as they grapple with the harsh realities of grief and loss.

As the days turn into weeks and months, the Salmon family's grief takes on a variety of forms, from anger and resentment to sadness and despair. Their once tight-knit family is strained to the breaking point as they struggle to come to terms with the reality of Susie's absence. Each member of the family copes with their grief in their own way, seeking solace in the memories of their lost loved one.

Throughout their journey, the Salmon family is buoyed by the support of their community, who rally around them in their time of need. Neighbors and friends offer words of comfort and acts of kindness, providing a glimmer of hope amidst the darkness of their grief. Together, they navigate the turbulent waters of loss, drawing strength from their shared experiences and the enduring bonds of love and friendship.

As the film progresses, the Salmon family's journey towards healing becomes increasingly intertwined with the search for Susie. Their quest for closure takes them to dark and unexpected places, forcing them to confront uncomfortable truths about their own lives and relationships. Along the way, they find solace in each other, forging new connections and rediscovering the power of love and forgiveness.

Ultimately, "A Family in Turmoil: Coping with Loss" serves as a poignant reminder of the resilience of the human spirit in the face of unimaginable tragedy. Through the lens of the Salmon family's experience, the film explores the complex and often painful process of grief and the transformative power of love and forgiveness. As they navigate the darkest moments of their grief, the Salmons emerge stronger and more resilient, honoring Susie's memory with each step they take forward.

The Afterlife Revealed

Susie's Journey Beyond

In "The Lovely Bones," the theme of the afterlife plays a significant role, especially through the perspective of Susie Salmon, the young protagonist whose life is tragically cut short. Heading 3, "The Afterlife Revealed: Susie's Journey Beyond," delves into the ethereal realm that Susie inhabits after her untimely death and explores how this dimension serves as a lens through which she processes her own emotions and observes the lives of those she left behind.

Susie's journey into the afterlife begins with a sense of confusion and disorientation. As her spirit transitions from the earthly realm to the ethereal plane, she finds herself in a place of beauty and tranquility, unlike anything she has ever experienced. This otherworldly realm, depicted with stunning visual imagery, serves as a stark contrast to the darkness and despair that surround her family and friends in the wake of her death.

As Susie navigates this new and unfamiliar landscape, she encounters other spirits who have passed on before her. These spectral beings, portrayed with a sense of otherworldly grace, serve as guides and companions on her journey, offering wisdom and insight as she grapples with the complexities of her own emotions.

One of the most poignant aspects of Susie's journey in the afterlife is her ability to observe the lives of those she left behind. From her heavenly vantage point, she watches as her family and friends struggle to come to terms with her death, each coping in their own way. Through her eyes, the audience gains insight into the inner thoughts and emotions of the characters, adding depth to their experiences and relationships.

Susie's observations from the afterlife serve as a powerful narrative device, allowing the audience to witness the impact of her death on those she loved. From her father's relentless quest for justice to her mother's descent into grief and despair, Susie bears witness to the full spectrum of human emotion in the wake of tragedy. Her presence, though intangible, serves as a source of comfort and solace for her family, guiding them through the darkest moments of their grief.

Throughout her journey in the afterlife, Susie grapples with feelings of anger, regret, and longing as she comes to terms with the reality of her own death. She mourns the loss of the life she never had the chance to live, lamenting the milestones and experiences that were stolen from her. Yet, amidst her sorrow, Susie finds moments of beauty and joy in the connections she forms with other spirits and the memories she cherishes from her time on earth.

One of the central themes of Susie's journey in the afterlife is the concept of closure and forgiveness. As she watches her family and friends struggle to move on in the wake of her death, Susie grapples with the idea of letting go and finding peace. Through her interactions with other spirits and her own introspection, she comes to understand the power of forgiveness and the importance of letting go of anger and resentment.

Susie's journey in the afterlife is ultimately a journey of self-discovery and acceptance. As she confronts the traumas of her past and the pain of her own death, she learns to embrace the beauty and fragility of life. Through her experiences in the afterlife, Susie gains a deeper understanding of herself and the world around her, finding solace in the knowledge that love endures beyond the boundaries of life and death.

In conclusion, "The Afterlife Revealed: Susie's Journey Beyond" serves as a poignant exploration of life, death, and the power of love to transcend the boundaries of mortality. Through the lens of Susie's journey in the afterlife, the film delves into the complexities of grief, forgiveness, and acceptance, offering a message of hope and redemption in the face of tragedy. As Susie navigates the ethereal realm and bears witness to the lives of those she left behind, she ultimately finds peace in the knowledge that her spirit will live on in the hearts of those who loved her.

Searching for Justice

Uncovering the Truth

In "The Lovely Bones," the quest for justice becomes a pivotal element following the disappearance of Susie Salmon. Heading 4, "Searching for Justice: Uncovering the Truth," encapsulates the relentless pursuit of truth and accountability undertaken by Susie's loved ones and the wider community as they seek to bring closure to the mystery surrounding her disappearance.

From the moment Susie goes missing, her family and friends are consumed by a desperate need for answers. Led by Susie's father, Jack Salmon, portrayed by Mark Wahlberg, they launch a tireless search for clues that might lead to her whereabouts. Their efforts are fueled by a potent mix of fear, anger, and determination, as they refuse to rest until the truth is revealed.

As the investigation unfolds, suspicion falls on George Harvey, a reclusive neighbor portrayed by Stanley Tucci, whose sinister demeanor and suspicious behavior cast a shadow of doubt over the tight-knit community. Harvey's unsettling presence becomes a focal point of the investigation, as the Salmons and their allies seek to uncover the truth behind Susie's disappearance.

The search for justice takes on a variety of forms, from traditional police work to clandestine investigations conducted by Susie's family and friends. Each clue, no matter how small, becomes a potential piece of the puzzle as they piece together the events leading up to Susie's disappearance. Their quest for justice becomes a testament to the power of love and determination in the face of overwhelming adversity.

As the investigation intensifies, tensions mount within the community, as neighbors and friends grapple with the unsettling realization that a predator may be living among them. Susie's disappearance serves as a wake-up call, forcing them to confront uncomfortable truths about the fragility of safety and security in their seemingly idyllic suburban neighborhood.

The search for justice becomes a deeply personal journey for Susie's family and friends, each driven by their own motivations and desires for closure. For Jack Salmon, it is a quest for redemption, as he seeks to make amends for his perceived failure to protect his daughter. For Abigail Salmon, portrayed by Rachel Weisz, it is a desperate attempt to find meaning amidst the chaos of grief and loss. And for Lindsey Salmon, played by Rose McIver, it is a fight for justice on behalf of her beloved sister, whose voice has been silenced by violence.

As the investigation reaches its climax, the truth about Susie's disappearance is finally revealed, sending shockwaves through the community and bringing a sense of closure to her loved ones. The revelation of Harvey's guilt serves as a bittersweet victory for the Salmons, offering a measure of vindication for their relentless pursuit of justice.

Yet, even as the truth is uncovered, the scars left behind by Susie's disappearance continue to linger, serving as a constant reminder of the fragility of life and the darkness that lurks beneath the surface of seemingly ordinary existence. The quest for justice may have brought closure to Susie's loved ones, but it cannot erase the pain of her absence or the trauma of her untimely death.

In the end, "Searching for Justice: Uncovering the Truth" serves as a testament to the resilience of the human spirit in the face of unimaginable tragedy. Through the lens of Susie's disappearance, the film explores the complexities of grief, loss, and the quest for justice, offering a message of hope and redemption in the face of overwhelming darkness. As Susie's loved ones grapple with the aftermath of her disappearance, they are ultimately united by their shared determination to honor her memory and find peace amidst the chaos of their shattered lives.

Glimpses of Hope

Healing Amidst Grief

In "The Lovely Bones," amidst the overwhelming darkness of grief and loss, there are moments of light and hope that emerge, guiding the characters on their journey towards healing. Heading 5, "Glimpses of Hope: Healing Amidst Grief," delves into these moments of resilience, redemption, and renewal that serve as beacons of light in the midst of profound darkness.

From the moment Susie Salmon goes missing, her family and friends are plunged into a world of unimaginable pain and despair. The weight of their grief threatens to consume them, leaving them adrift in a sea of uncertainty and sorrow. Yet, amidst the darkness, there are glimpses of hope that emerge, offering moments of solace and comfort in the face of overwhelming adversity.

One of the most profound sources of hope in the film is the resilience of the human spirit. Despite the crushing weight of grief, Susie's loved ones refuse to succumb to despair, finding strength in their shared memories and the enduring bonds of love that unite them. Their resilience serves as a powerful reminder of the indomitable nature of the human spirit, capable of weathering even the most devastating of storms.

Throughout the film, acts of kindness and compassion emerge as beacons of hope in the darkness. From the support of friends and neighbors to the selfless sacrifices made by loved ones, these acts of kindness serve as reminders of the inherent goodness that exists within humanity. In the midst of tragedy, they offer moments of connection and solidarity, reaffirming the belief that even in the darkest of times, love and compassion can prevail.

One of the most poignant sources of hope in the film is the journey of healing undertaken by Susie's family. In the wake of her disappearance, each member of the Salmon family grapples with their own unique journey towards acceptance and healing. Jack Salmon, Susie's father, finds solace in his relentless pursuit of justice, channeling his grief into a quest for redemption. Abigail Salmon, Susie's mother, confronts her grief head-on, embarking on a journey of self-discovery and forgiveness. And Lindsey Salmon, Susie's sister, finds strength in her determination to uncover the truth about what happened to her sister, refusing to let her memory fade into obscurity.

As the film progresses, these individual journeys towards healing converge, leading to moments of profound catharsis and redemption. Jack finds closure in his quest for justice, finally able to let go of the guilt and anger that have consumed him since Susie's disappearance. Abigail confronts her grief and guilt head-on, finding peace in the knowledge that she did everything she could to protect her daughter. And Lindsey emerges from the darkness stronger and more resilient than ever, honoring her sister's memory with each step she takes forward.

Another source of hope in the film is the enduring power of love to transcend the boundaries of life and death. Despite the physical absence of Susie, her presence continues to be felt by her loved ones, guiding them through the darkest moments of their grief. Through their shared memories and the legacy of love that Susie leaves behind, her family and friends find comfort and solace, knowing that she will always be with them in spirit.

Ultimately, "Glimpses of Hope: Healing Amidst Grief" serves as a testament to the resilience of the human spirit and the transformative power of love and compassion in the face of overwhelming adversity. Through the lens of Susie's disappearance, the film explores the complexities of grief, loss, and the journey towards healing, offering a message of hope and redemption in the face of profound darkness. As Susie's loved ones navigate the tumultuous waters of grief, they are ultimately united by their shared determination to honor her memory and find peace amidst the chaos of their shattered lives.

The Bonds of Love

Family Dynamics in Crisis

In "The Lovely Bones," the bonds of love are put to the ultimate test in the face of unimaginable tragedy. Heading 6, "The Bonds of Love: Family Dynamics in Crisis," delves into the intricate dynamics of the Salmon family as they grapple with the profound loss of their beloved daughter and sister, Susie. Through their journey of grief, each member of the family is forced to confront their own vulnerabilities, strengths, and the complexities of their relationships.

At the heart of the Salmon family is Jack Salmon, the patriarch portrayed by Mark Wahlberg. Jack embodies the quintessential image of a loving and devoted father, whose world is shattered when Susie goes missing. His initial reaction to Susie's disappearance is one of frantic desperation, as he launches a relentless search to find her, clinging to hope even as the days turn into weeks and months. Jack's unwavering determination to find his daughter serves as a driving force throughout the film, propelling him forward in the face of overwhelming despair.

Abigail Salmon, Susie's mother, portrayed by Rachel Weisz, is a complex and multifaceted character whose journey through grief is fraught with emotional turmoil. Abigail's initial reaction to Susie's disappearance is one of shock and disbelief, followed by a deep and profound sense of grief. Consumed by guilt and remorse, she retreats into herself, unable to find solace in the familiar routines of everyday life. Abigail's journey through grief is one of profound transformation, as she confronts her own vulnerabilities and finds the strength to move forward in the face of overwhelming darkness.

Lindsey Salmon, Susie's younger sister, portrayed by Rose McIver, serves as a beacon of hope and resilience in the midst of tragedy. Initially grappling with feelings of anger and resentment towards her sister, Lindsey's journey towards acceptance is one of profound growth and self-discovery. As she learns to navigate the complexities of grief, Lindsey emerges stronger and more resilient than ever, honoring Susie's memory with each step she takes forward.

Buckley Salmon, the youngest member of the family, is also deeply affected by Susie's disappearance, despite his inability to fully comprehend the magnitude of the tragedy. Buckley's innocence serves as a poignant reminder of the impact that Susie's loss has on the entire family, as they struggle to come to terms with the reality of her absence.

As the film progresses, the bonds of love that unite the Salmon family are tested in ways they never could have imagined. Each member of the family copes with their grief in their own way, navigating the turbulent waters of loss and despair. Yet, amidst the darkness, there are moments of light and connection that emerge, offering glimpses of hope amidst the overwhelming pain.

One of the most poignant moments in the film comes when Jack and Abigail confront their own vulnerabilities and shortcomings as parents. In a heartbreaking scene, they come to realize that their inability to communicate effectively with one another has contributed to the breakdown of their family unit. Yet, even in the midst of their pain, they find solace in the knowledge that their love for one another and for Susie transcends the boundaries of life and death.

Throughout their journey of grief, the Salmon family is buoyed by the support of their community, who rally around them in their time of need. Neighbors and friends offer words of comfort and acts of kindness, serving as a reminder of the power of love and compassion to heal even the deepest wounds.

Ultimately, "The Bonds of Love: Family Dynamics in Crisis" serves as a poignant exploration of the resilience of the human spirit and the transformative power of love in the face of unimaginable tragedy. Through the lens of the Salmon family's experience, the film explores the complexities of grief, loss, and the journey towards healing, offering a message of hope and redemption in the face of profound darkness. As the Salmons navigate the tumultuous waters of grief, they are ultimately united by their shared determination to honor Susie's memory and find peace amidst the chaos of their shattered lives.

A Father's Quest

Seeking Redemption

In "The Lovely Bones," the character of Jack Salmon, portrayed by Mark Wahlberg, embarks on a profound and relentless quest for redemption following the disappearance of his daughter, Susie. Heading 7, "A Father's Quest: Seeking Redemption," delves into Jack's journey as he grapples with the overwhelming guilt and anguish that accompany the loss of his beloved daughter, and his unwavering determination to find justice and closure.

From the moment Susie goes missing, Jack's world is shattered. As a loving and devoted father, he is consumed by a sense of responsibility for his daughter's safety and well-being. His initial reaction to Susie's disappearance is one of frantic desperation, as he launches a tireless search to find her, clinging to hope even as the days turn into weeks and months. Jack's unwavering determination to find his daughter serves as a driving force throughout the film, propelling him forward in the face of overwhelming despair.

Yet, amidst his quest for justice, Jack is haunted by a profound sense of guilt and remorse. He blames himself for Susie's disappearance, tortured by the belief that he failed to protect his daughter when she needed him most. This guilt consumes him, driving a wedge between himself and his family as he becomes increasingly consumed by his single-minded pursuit of justice.

As the investigation into Susie's disappearance unfolds, Jack's quest for redemption becomes increasingly intertwined with his desire for closure. He becomes obsessed with finding the truth, convinced that uncovering the identity of Susie's killer will somehow absolve him of his guilt and allow him to find peace. His relentless pursuit of justice becomes a desperate attempt to make amends for his perceived failure as a father, as he seeks redemption for the sins of the past.

Throughout his journey, Jack is forced to confront uncomfortable truths about himself and his family. He grapples with his own vulnerabilities and shortcomings as a parent, coming to realize that his inability to communicate effectively with his wife, Abigail, has contributed to the breakdown of their family unit. Yet, even in the midst of his pain, Jack finds solace in the knowledge that his love for his daughter and his unwavering determination to find justice will never waver.

One of the most poignant moments in the film comes when Jack confronts Susie's killer, George Harvey, portrayed by Stanley Tucci. In a powerful and emotional confrontation, Jack comes face to face with the man responsible for his daughter's death, unleashing a torrent of pent-up rage and anguish. Yet, even in the midst of his fury, Jack finds a sense of catharsis in finally confronting the source of his pain, as he seeks to bring closure to the chapter of his life that has been defined by grief and despair.

As the film reaches its climax, Jack's quest for redemption culminates in a moment of profound catharsis. In the aftermath of Susie's killer being brought to justice, Jack finds a sense of closure that has long eluded him. Though the pain of his daughter's loss will never fully fade, he is able to find peace in the knowledge that he did everything he could to find justice for her.

Ultimately, "A Father's Quest: Seeking Redemption" serves as a poignant exploration of the depths of parental love and the lengths to which a father will go to protect his child. Through the lens of Jack's journey, the film explores the complexities of guilt, grief, and the quest for redemption, offering a message of hope and healing in the face of profound darkness. As Jack navigates the tumultuous waters of grief, he is ultimately able to find redemption in the love he shared with his daughter and the justice he fought tirelessly to achieve.

The Perils of Obsession

Suspects Unmasked

In "The Lovely Bones," the theme of obsession takes center stage as Susie's family and community grapple with the unsettling reality of her disappearance. Heading 8, "The Perils of Obsession: Suspects Unmasked," delves into the various characters who become consumed by their fixation on finding Susie's killer, and the dangers that arise when their obsessions threaten to consume them.

At the heart of the investigation into Susie's disappearance is George Harvey, a reclusive neighbor portrayed by Stanley Tucci. From the moment Susie goes missing, Harvey becomes a prime suspect in the eyes of the community, his suspicious behavior and unsettling demeanor casting a shadow of doubt over the tight-knit suburban neighborhood. As the investigation unfolds, Harvey's obsession with evading capture becomes increasingly apparent, as he goes to great lengths to conceal his guilt and manipulate those around him.

Yet, Harvey is not the only character whose obsession threatens to consume them. Susie's father, Jack Salmon, portrayed by Mark Wahlberg, becomes consumed by his relentless quest for justice, his single-minded fixation on finding Susie's killer driving a wedge between himself and his family. His obsession with uncovering the truth becomes all-consuming, as he sacrifices his own well-being and the well-being of those around him in pursuit of closure.

Abigail Salmon, Susie's mother, portrayed by Rachel Weisz, also grapples with her own obsession in the wake of her daughter's disappearance. Consumed by grief and guilt, Abigail becomes fixated on finding a sense of closure, her desperate search for answers leading her down a path of self-destruction. Her obsession threatens to tear her family apart, as she becomes increasingly isolated and withdrawn, unable to find solace in the familiar routines of everyday life.

As the investigation into Susie's disappearance intensifies, tensions within the community reach a boiling point, as neighbors and friends grapple with the unsettling realization that a predator may be living among them. Suspicions run rampant, and accusations fly as the community becomes consumed by fear and paranoia. In the midst of the chaos, Harvey's obsession with maintaining his facade becomes increasingly desperate, as he resorts to increasingly drastic measures to avoid detection.

Throughout the film, the dangers of obsession are laid bare, as characters grapple with the consequences of their relentless pursuit of closure. Jack's obsession with finding Susie's killer leads him to neglect his own well-being and the well-being of his family, as he becomes consumed by his quest for justice. Abigail's obsession with finding closure threatens to tear her family apart, as she becomes increasingly isolated and withdrawn in the wake of her daughter's disappearance.

One of the most poignant moments in the film comes when Jack confronts Susie's killer, George Harvey, in a powerful and emotional confrontation. In a moment of profound catharsis, Jack unleashes a torrent of pent-up rage and anguish, confronting the source of his pain head-on. Yet, even in the midst of his fury, Jack comes to realize the dangers of obsession, as he grapples with the realization that his relentless quest for justice has come at a great cost.

As the film reaches its climax, the true dangers of obsession are laid bare, as characters confront the consequences of their actions. Harvey's obsession with evading capture ultimately leads to his downfall, as he is finally unmasked as Susie's killer and brought to justice. Yet, even in the moment of his capture, the scars left behind by his obsession continue to linger, serving as a reminder of the profound impact that obsession can have on those it consumes.

Ultimately, "The Perils of Obsession: Suspects Unmasked" serves as a cautionary tale about the dangers of allowing obsession to consume us. Through the lens of the characters' experiences, the film explores the complexities of guilt, grief, and the relentless pursuit of closure, offering a message of hope and redemption in the face of overwhelming darkness. As the characters grapple with the consequences of their actions, they ultimately come to realize the true cost of obsession, and the importance of finding balance in the pursuit of justice and closure.

Healing Through Connection

Community Support

In "The Lovely Bones," the importance of community support emerges as a central theme in the aftermath of Susie Salmon's disappearance. Heading 9, "Healing Through Connection: Community Support," delves into the ways in which the tight-knit suburban neighborhood rallies together in the face of tragedy, offering comfort, solace, and strength to Susie's family and friends as they navigate the tumultuous waters of grief.

From the moment Susie goes missing, the community is thrust into a state of shock and disbelief. The once serene suburban neighborhood is transformed into a place haunted by fear and uncertainty, as residents grapple with the unsettling realization that a predator may be living among them. Yet, amidst the darkness, there are glimmers of light that emerge, as neighbors and friends come together to offer support and assistance to Susie's family in their time of need.

One of the most poignant aspects of community support in the film is the way in which neighbors and friends rally around the Salmon family in the aftermath of Susie's disappearance. From the moment the news breaks, the community springs into action, organizing search parties, distributing flyers, and offering words of comfort and encouragement to Jack, Abigail, and their other children, Lindsey and Buckley. The outpouring of support serves as a powerful reminder of the resilience of the human spirit in the face of tragedy, as neighbors and friends come together to offer strength and solace to those in need.

Throughout the film, acts of kindness and compassion abound as the community bands together to support the Salmon family in their time of need. From homemade meals and heartfelt condolences to offers of assistance and acts of solidarity, the community's response to Susie's disappearance serves as a testament to the power of love and compassion to transcend even the darkest of times. In the midst of their grief, the Salmons find comfort in the knowledge that they are not alone, as they are surrounded by a community that cares deeply for them and shares in their sorrow.

One of the most poignant moments of community support in the film comes when Susie's classmates come together to pay tribute to their missing friend. In a heartfelt gesture of solidarity, they create a makeshift memorial in Susie's honor, adorning her locker with flowers, photographs, and heartfelt messages of love and remembrance. The outpouring of support from Susie's peers serves as a powerful reminder of the impact that she had on those around her, as classmates come together to mourn her loss and celebrate her memory.

As the investigation into Susie's disappearance unfolds, the community's response serves as a source of strength and inspiration to those involved. From law enforcement officials and volunteers to neighbors and friends, the entire community bands together to support the search for Susie and bring closure to her family. Their collective efforts serve as a testament to the power of unity and solidarity in the face of adversity, as they work tirelessly to find answers and seek justice for Susie and her loved ones.

Throughout the film, the importance of community support in the healing process is evident as the Salmons and their friends come to realize that they are not alone in their grief. From the initial shock of Susie's disappearance to the final moments of closure, the community stands by their side, offering comfort, strength, and solace as they navigate the tumultuous waters of grief and loss. In the end, "Healing Through Connection: Community Support" serves as a poignant reminder of the resilience of the human spirit and the transformative power of love and compassion in the face of tragedy.

Closure and Acceptance

Finding Peace in the Aftermath

In "The Lovely Bones," the theme of closure and acceptance emerges as a central focus as the characters navigate the aftermath of Susie Salmon's disappearance. Heading 10, "Closure and Acceptance: Finding Peace in the Aftermath," delves into the journey of the Salmon family and their community as they grapple with the harsh realities of grief and loss, ultimately finding solace and peace amidst the chaos of their shattered lives.

From the moment Susie goes missing, the quest for closure becomes a driving force for her family and friends. Each member of the Salmon family copes with their grief in their own way, navigating the complex and often tumultuous emotions that accompany such a profound tragedy. Yet, amidst the darkness, there are moments of light and hope that emerge, offering glimpses of peace and acceptance in the wake of overwhelming despair.

For Jack Salmon, Susie's father, portrayed by Mark Wahlberg, closure becomes synonymous with justice. From the moment Susie disappears, Jack becomes consumed by his relentless quest to find her killer, clinging to the hope that uncovering the truth will somehow bring him peace. His unwavering determination to find justice becomes a driving force throughout the film, propelling him forward in the face of overwhelming despair. Yet, as the investigation unfolds and Susie's killer is finally unmasked, Jack comes to realize that closure cannot be found in revenge or retribution. True closure, he discovers, lies in forgiveness and acceptance, as he learns to let go of the guilt and anger that have consumed him since Susie's disappearance.

Abigail Salmon, Susie's mother, portrayed by Rachel Weisz, also grapples with her own journey towards closure and acceptance. Consumed by grief and guilt, Abigail becomes fixated on finding a sense of closure, her desperate search for answers leading her down a path of self-destruction. Yet, as she confronts her own vulnerabilities and shortcomings, Abigail comes to realize that closure cannot be found in the past. True closure, she discovers, lies in embracing the present moment and finding peace amidst the chaos of grief and loss.

Lindsey Salmon, Susie's younger sister, portrayed by Rose McIver, also embarks on her own journey towards closure and acceptance. Initially grappling with feelings of anger and resentment towards her sister, Lindsey's journey towards acceptance is one of profound growth and self-discovery. As she learns to navigate the complexities of grief, Lindsey emerges stronger and more resilient than ever, honoring Susie's memory with each step she takes forward. Yet, as the truth about Susie's disappearance is finally revealed, Lindsey comes to realize that closure cannot be found in answers alone. True closure, she discovers, lies in embracing the love and memories that she shared with her sister, finding solace in the knowledge that Susie will always be with her in spirit.

As the film reaches its climax, the characters come to realize that closure is not a destination, but rather a journey. True closure, they discover, lies not in finding answers or seeking revenge, but in embracing the present moment and finding peace amidst the chaos of grief and loss. As they confront their own vulnerabilities and shortcomings, the characters find strength in their shared experiences and the enduring bonds of love and friendship that unite them. In the end, "Closure and Acceptance: Finding Peace in the Aftermath" serves as a poignant reminder of the resilience of the human spirit and the transformative power of love and forgiveness in the face of unimaginable tragedy. As the characters navigate the tumultuous waters of grief, they ultimately find solace and peace in the knowledge that their loved ones will always be with them in spirit, guiding them through the darkest moments of their lives.

The End

Printed in Great Britain
by Amazon